Cars & Trucks
A Coloring Experience

Copyright © 2024 RW Arts & Crafts
ISBN: 9798334684140

This Coloring Experience Belongs To:

Color Testing

Use the space below to test colors before using on your pictures

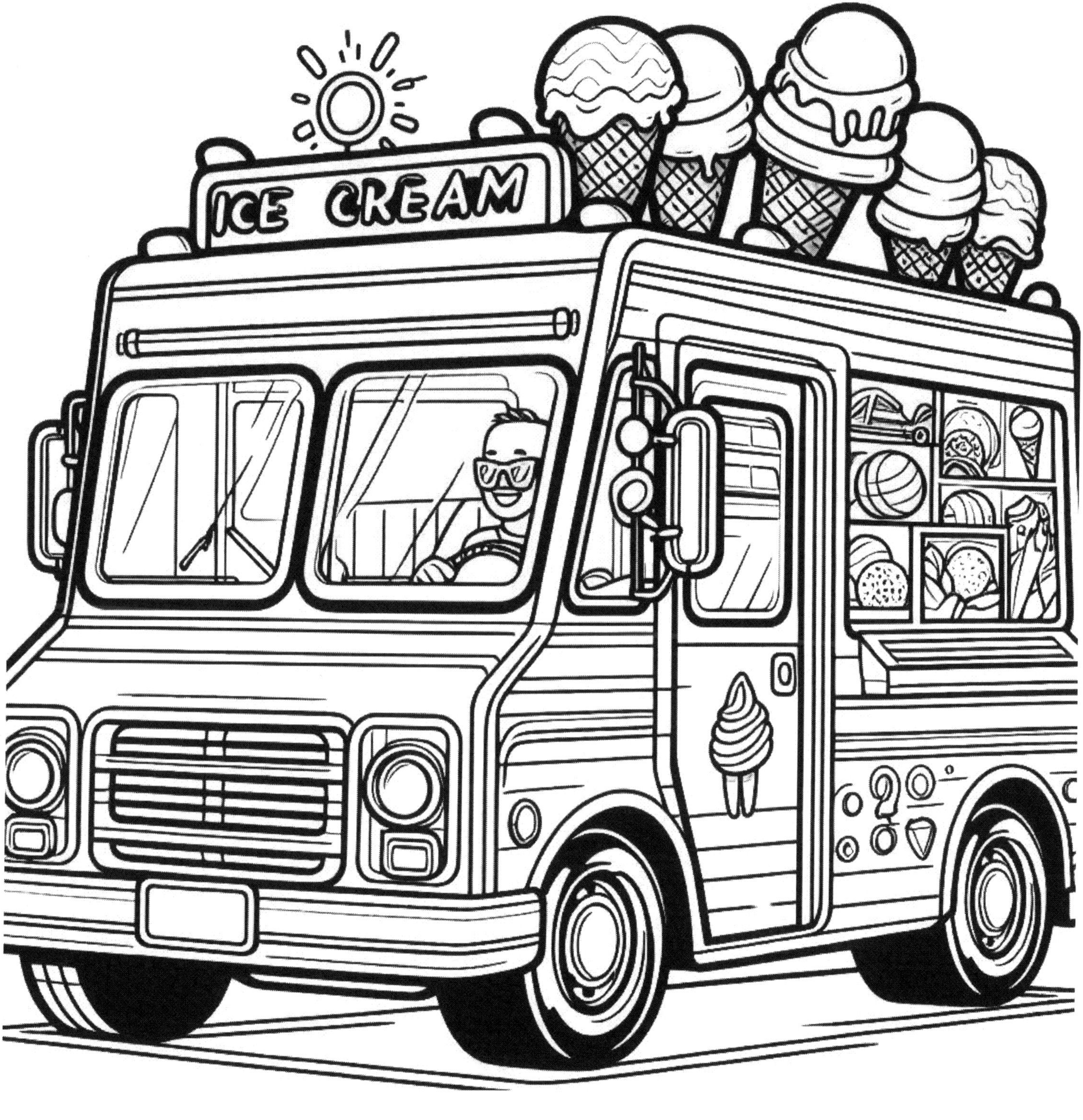
ICE CREAM

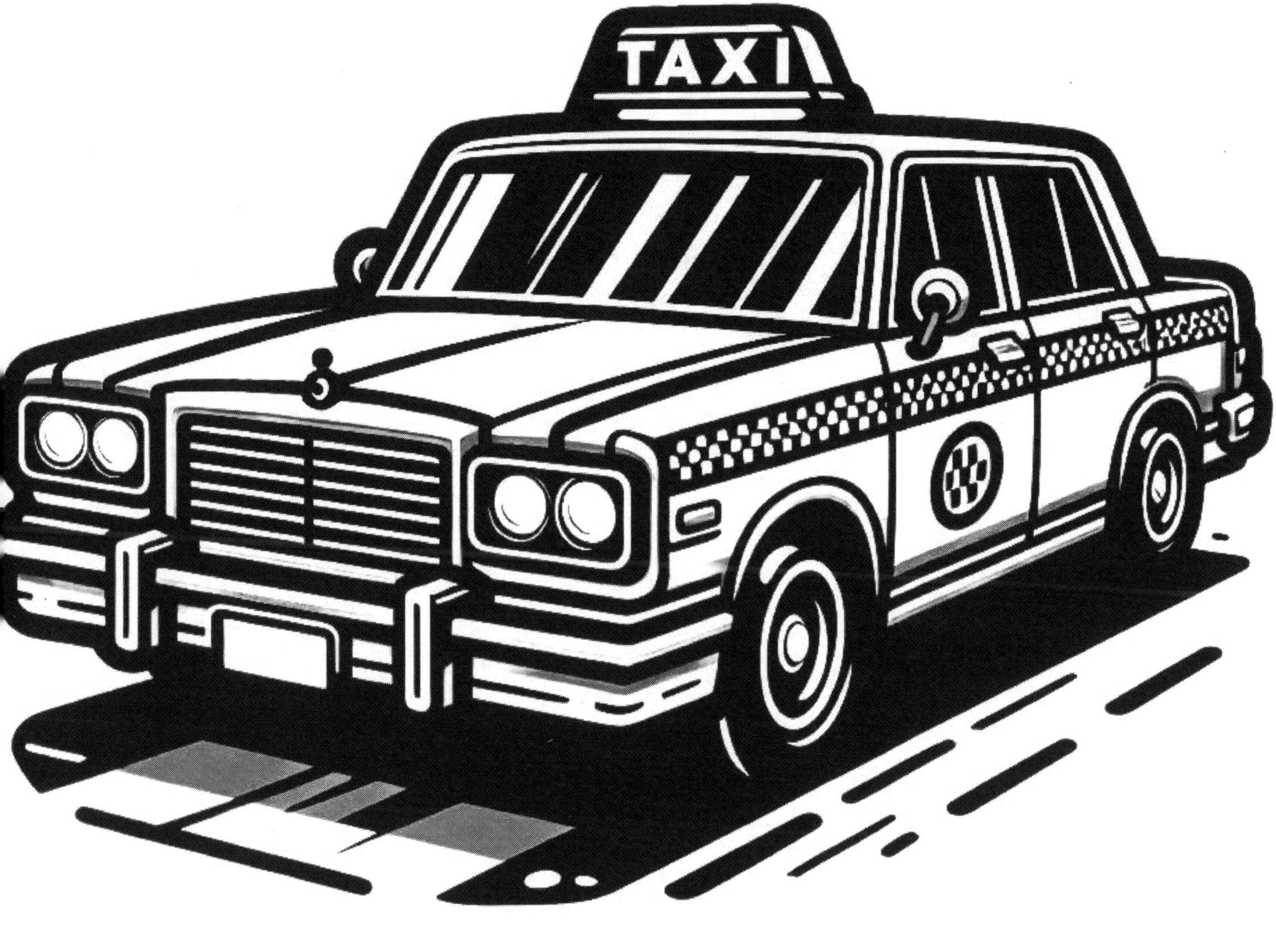
TAXI

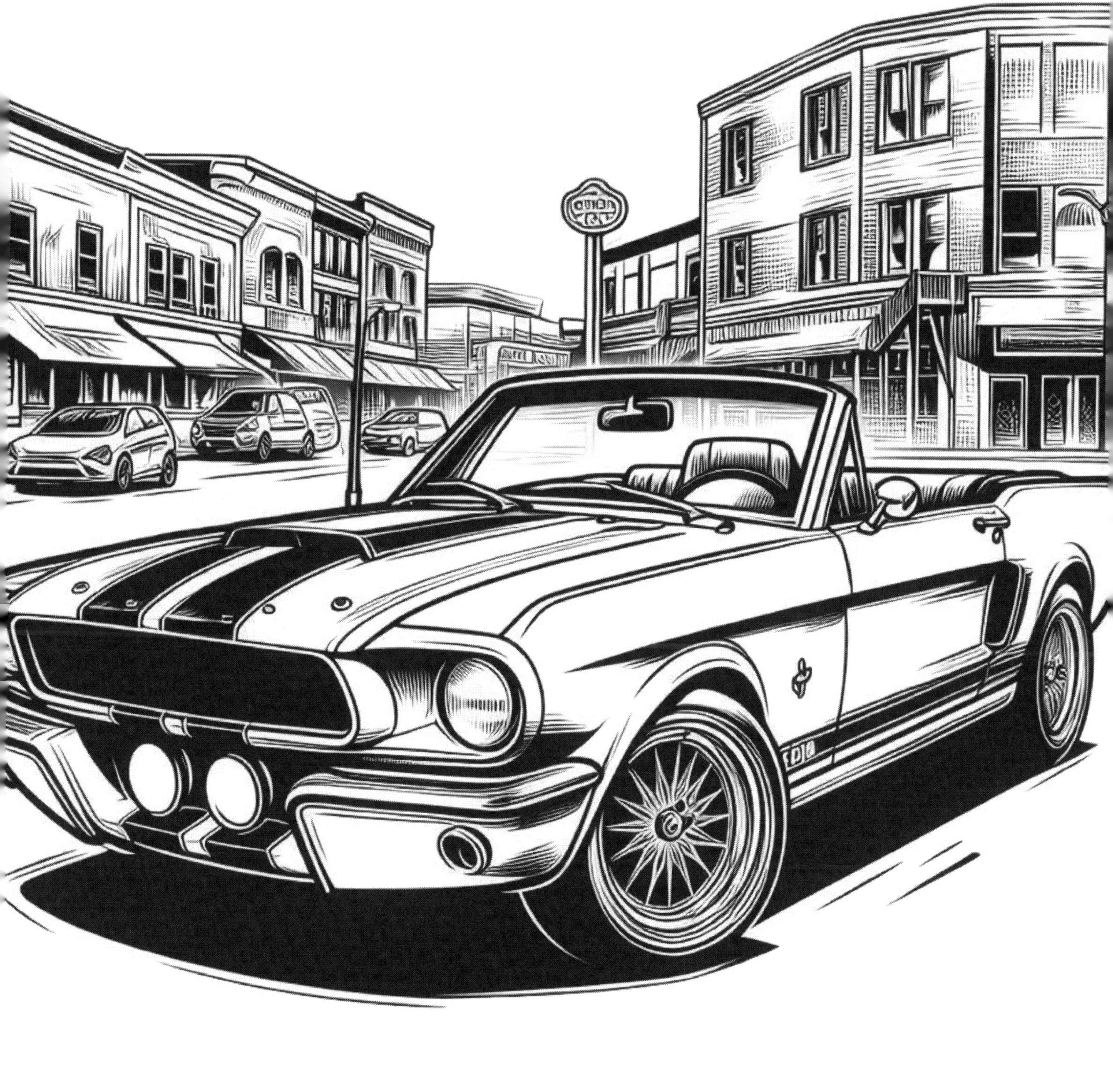

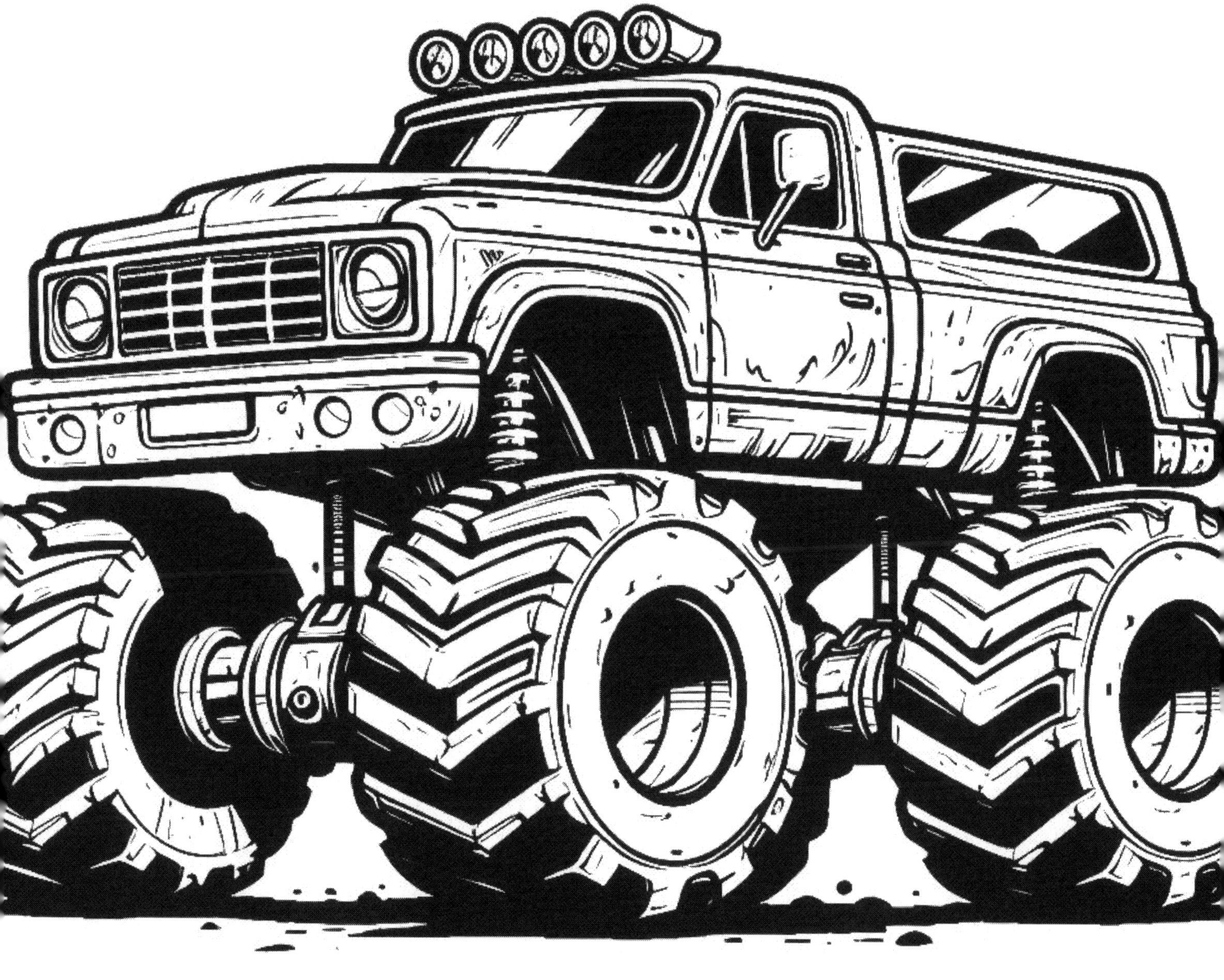

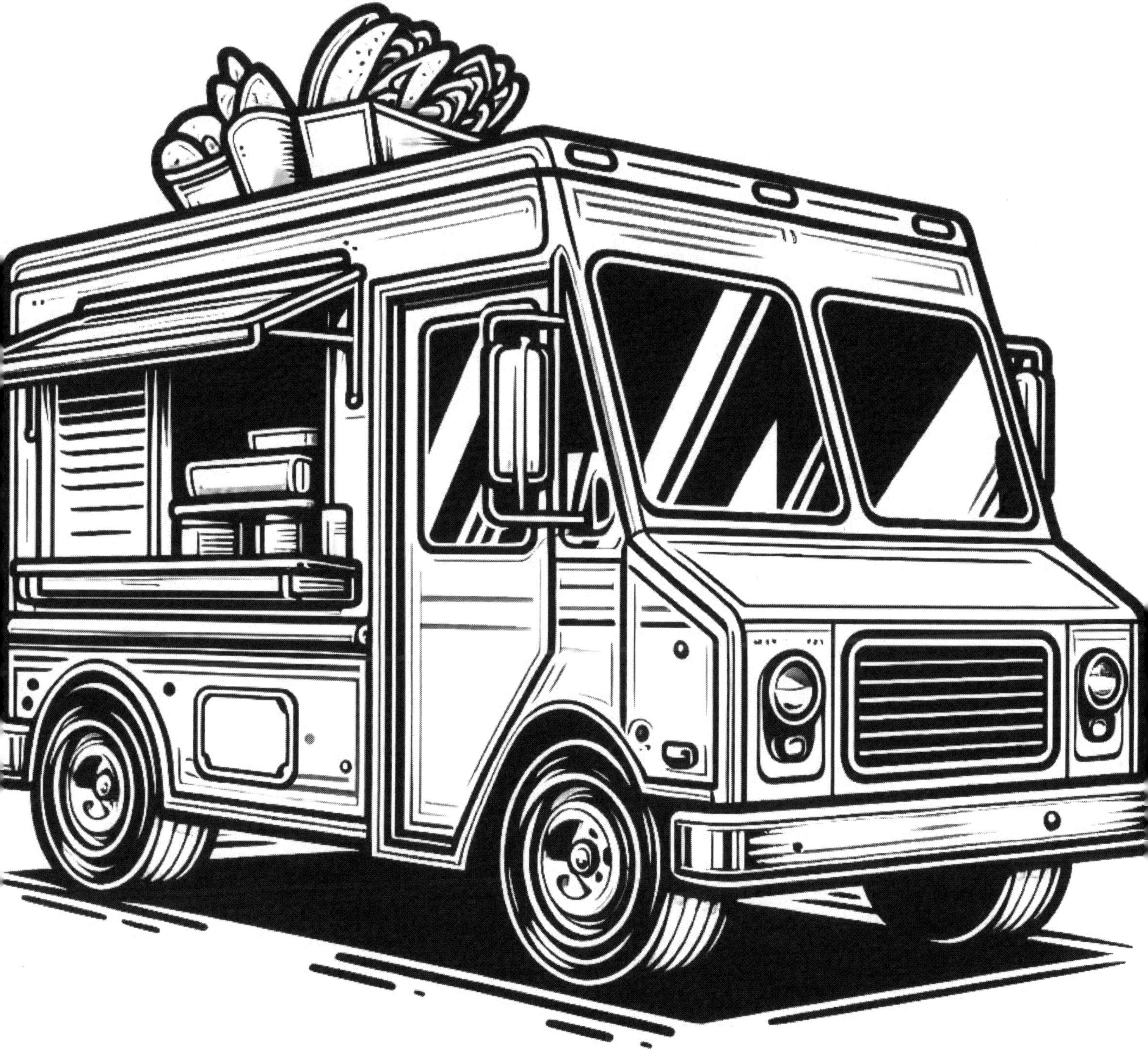

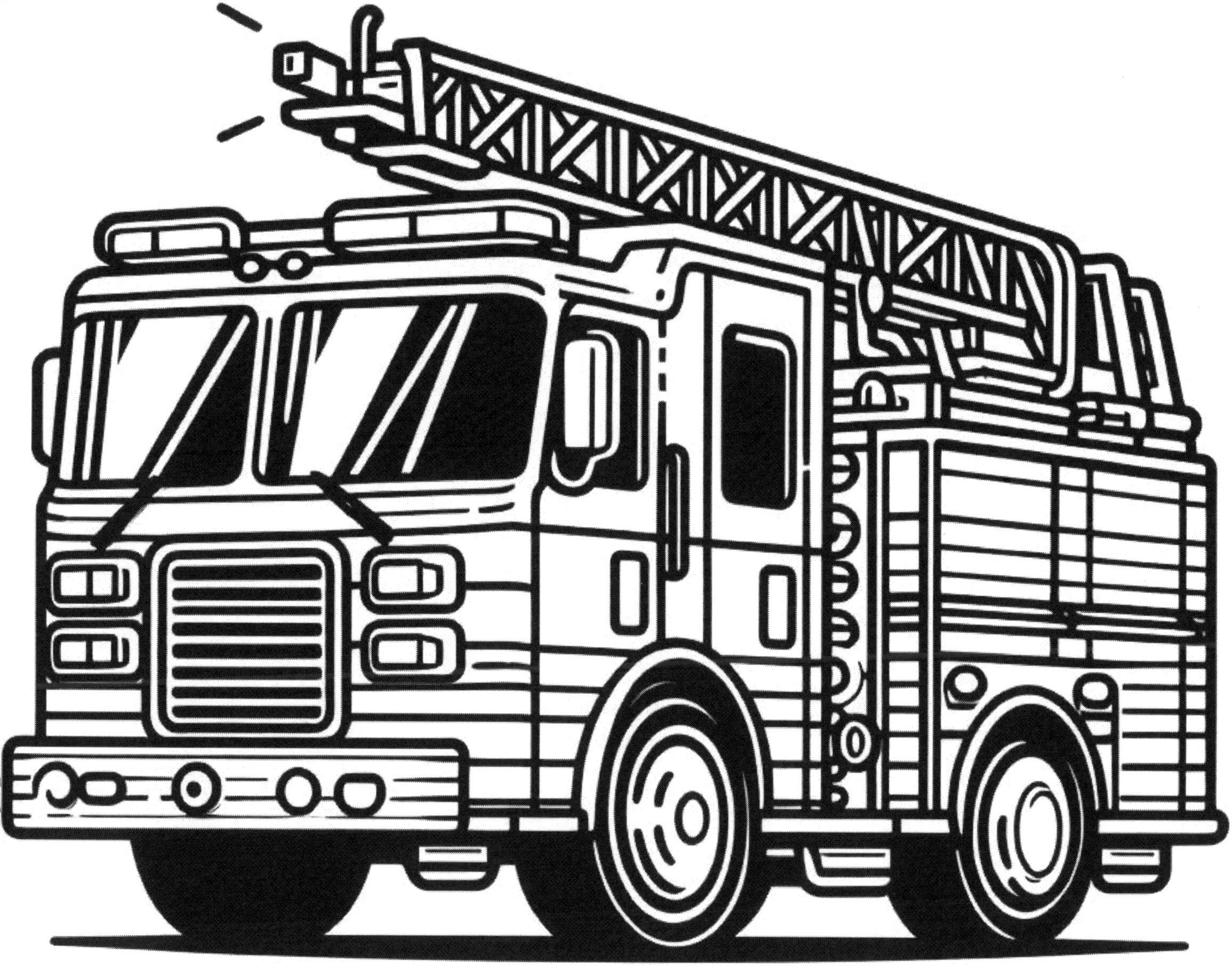

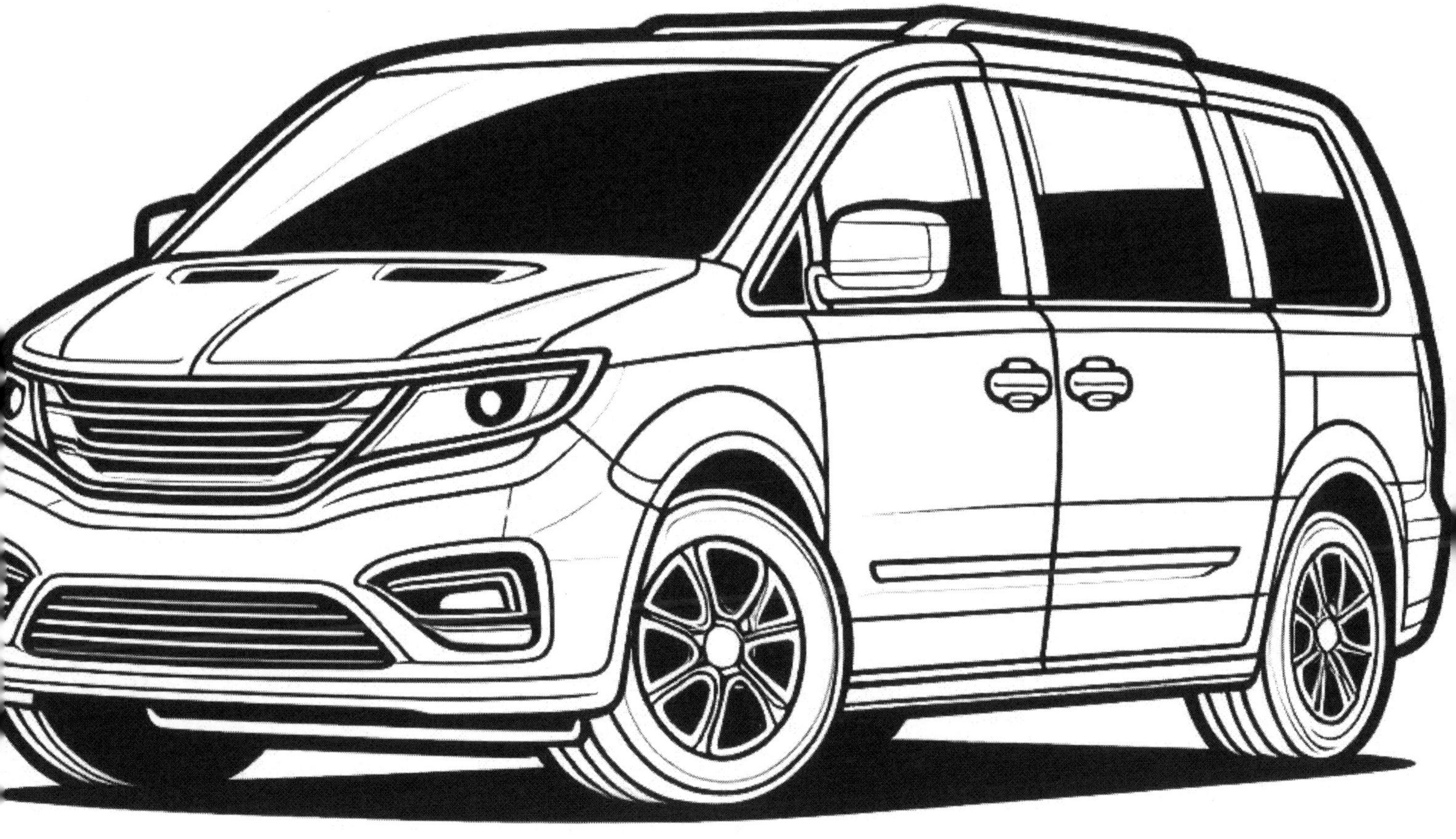

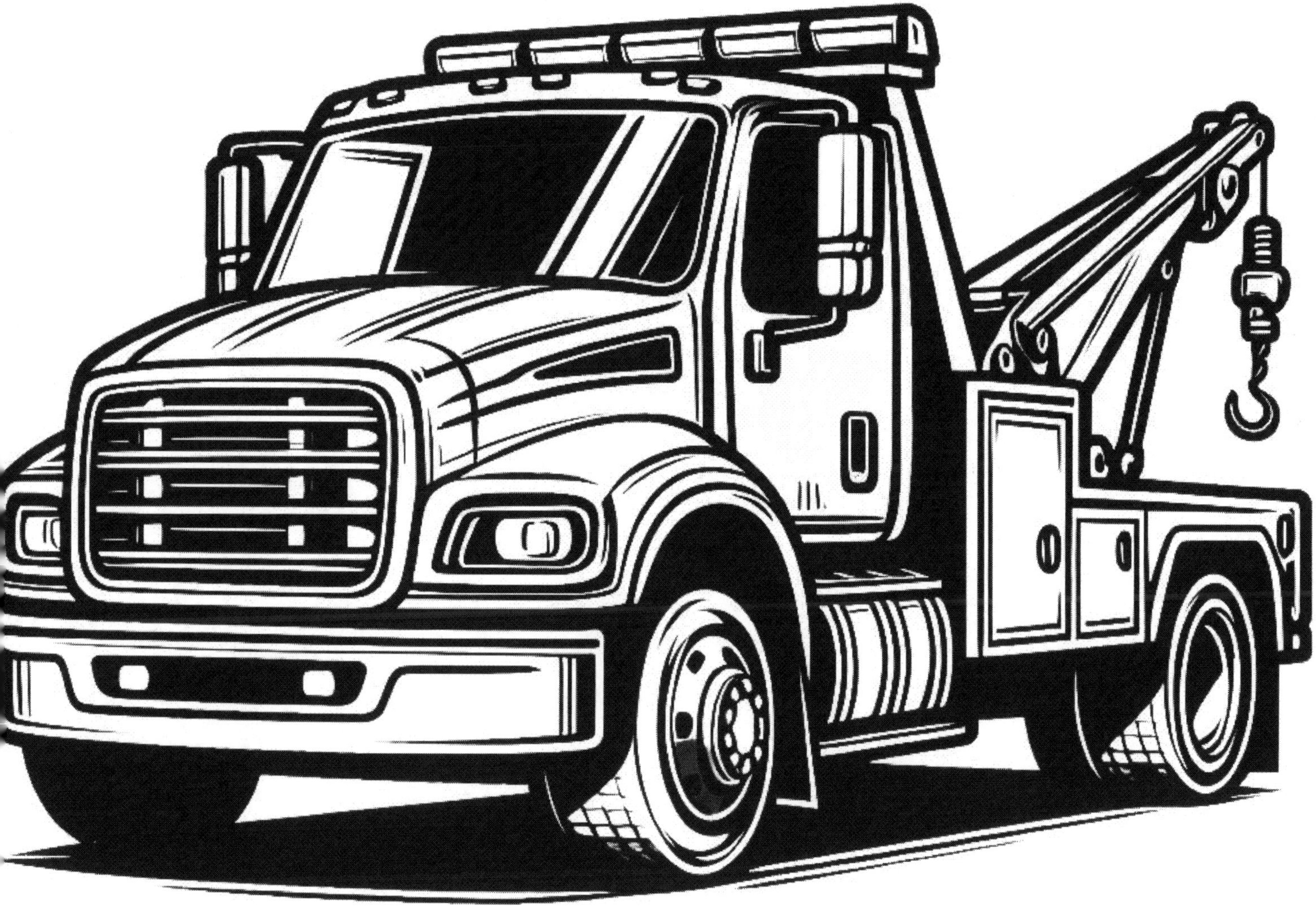

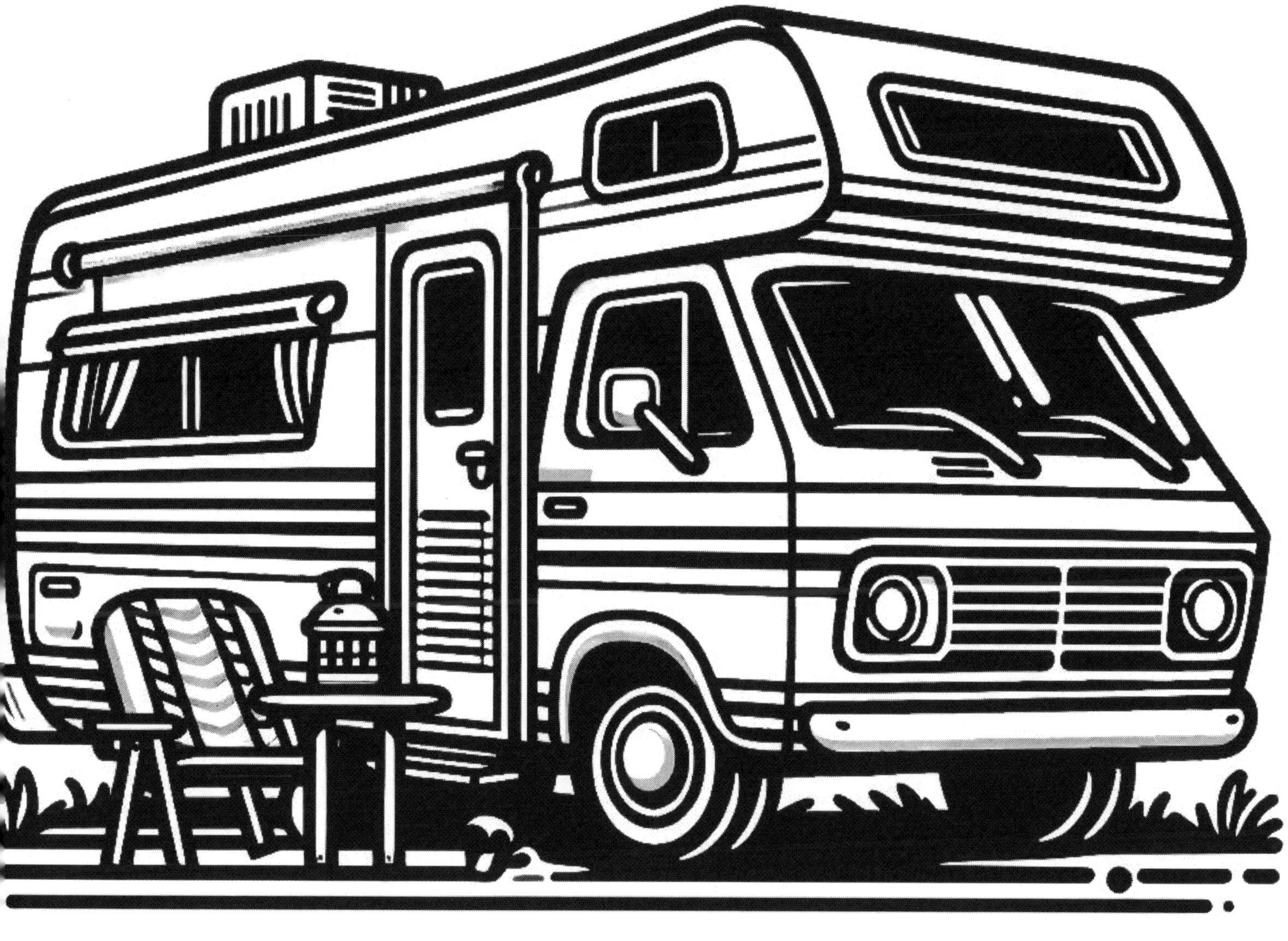

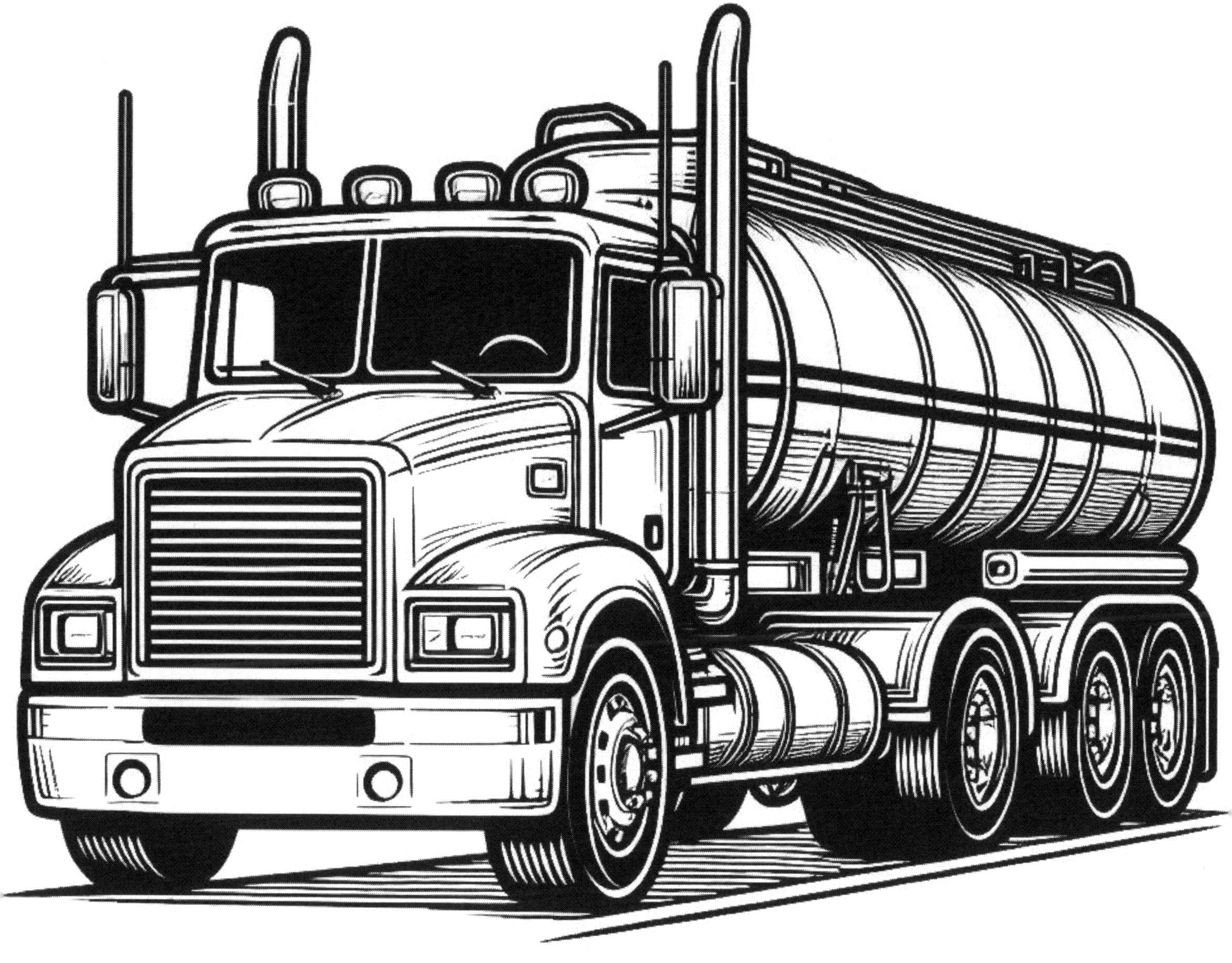

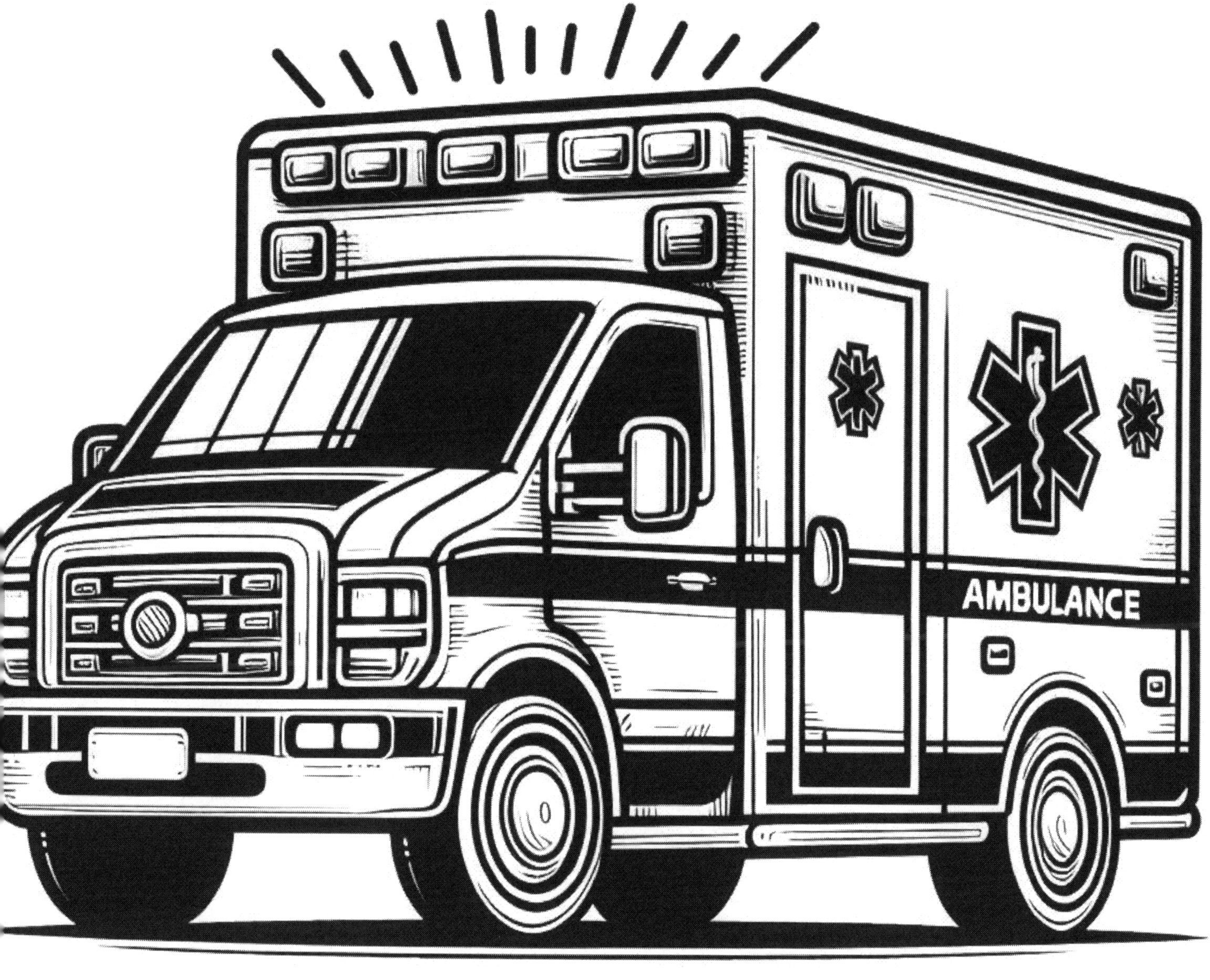
AMBULANCE

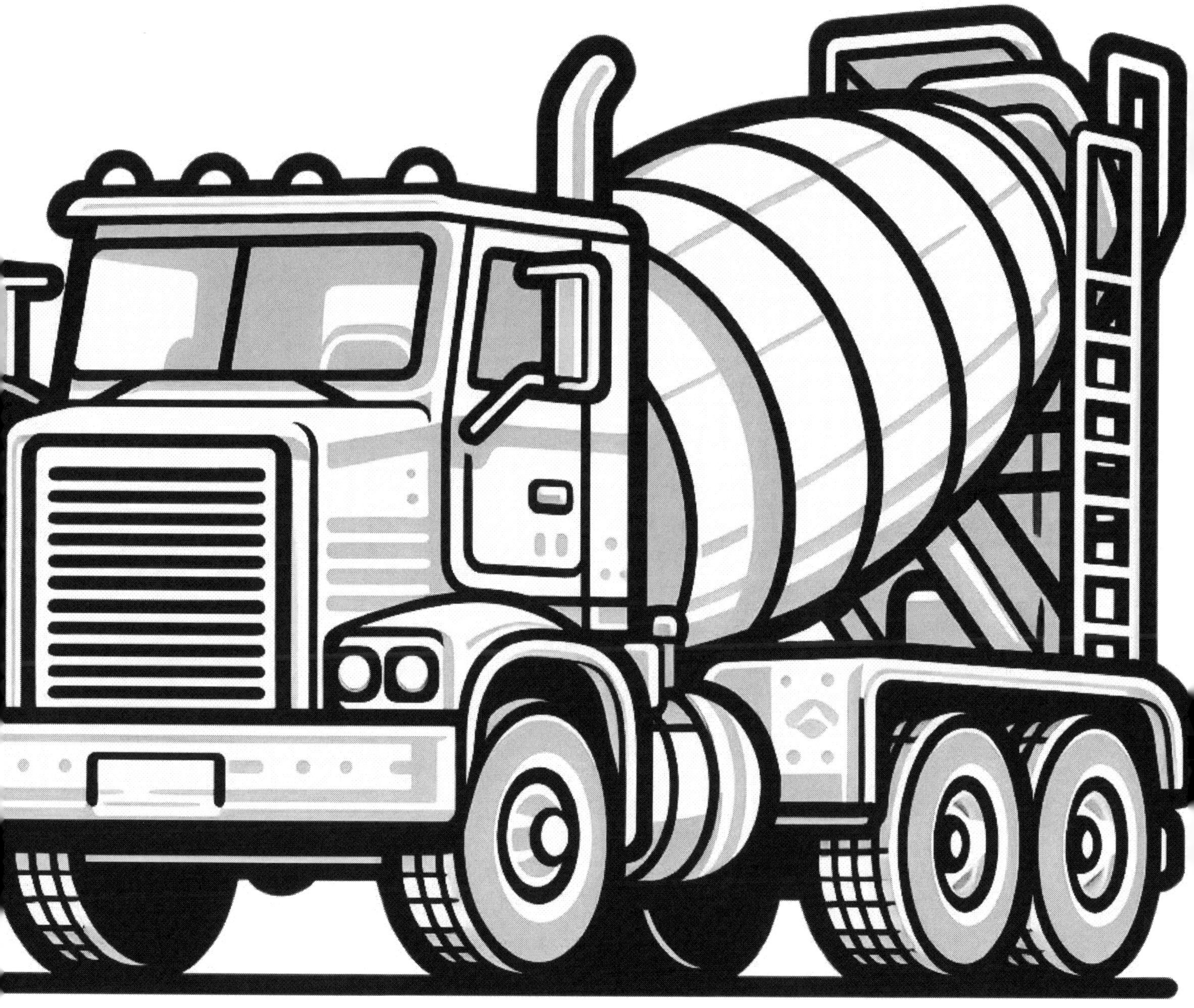

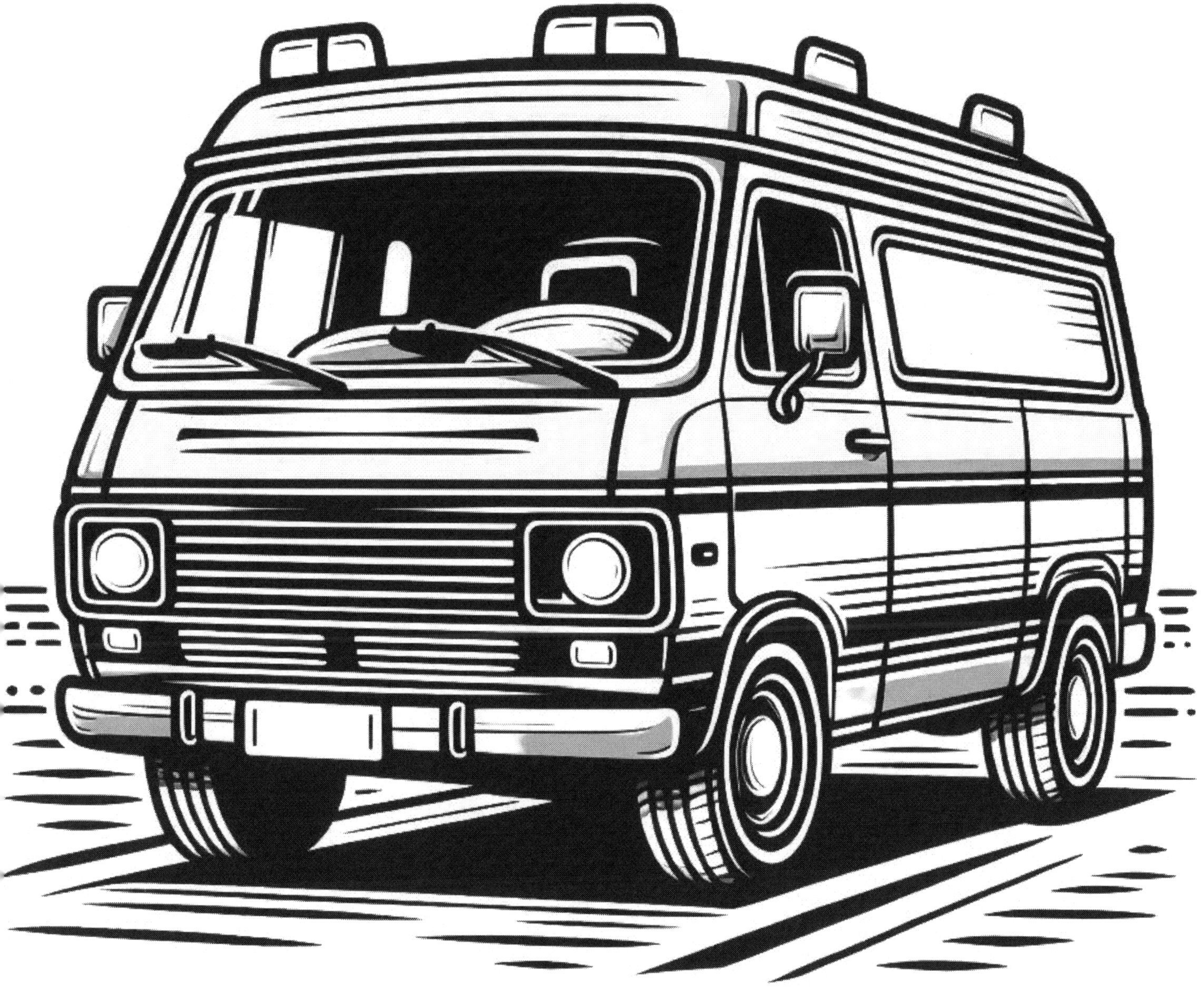

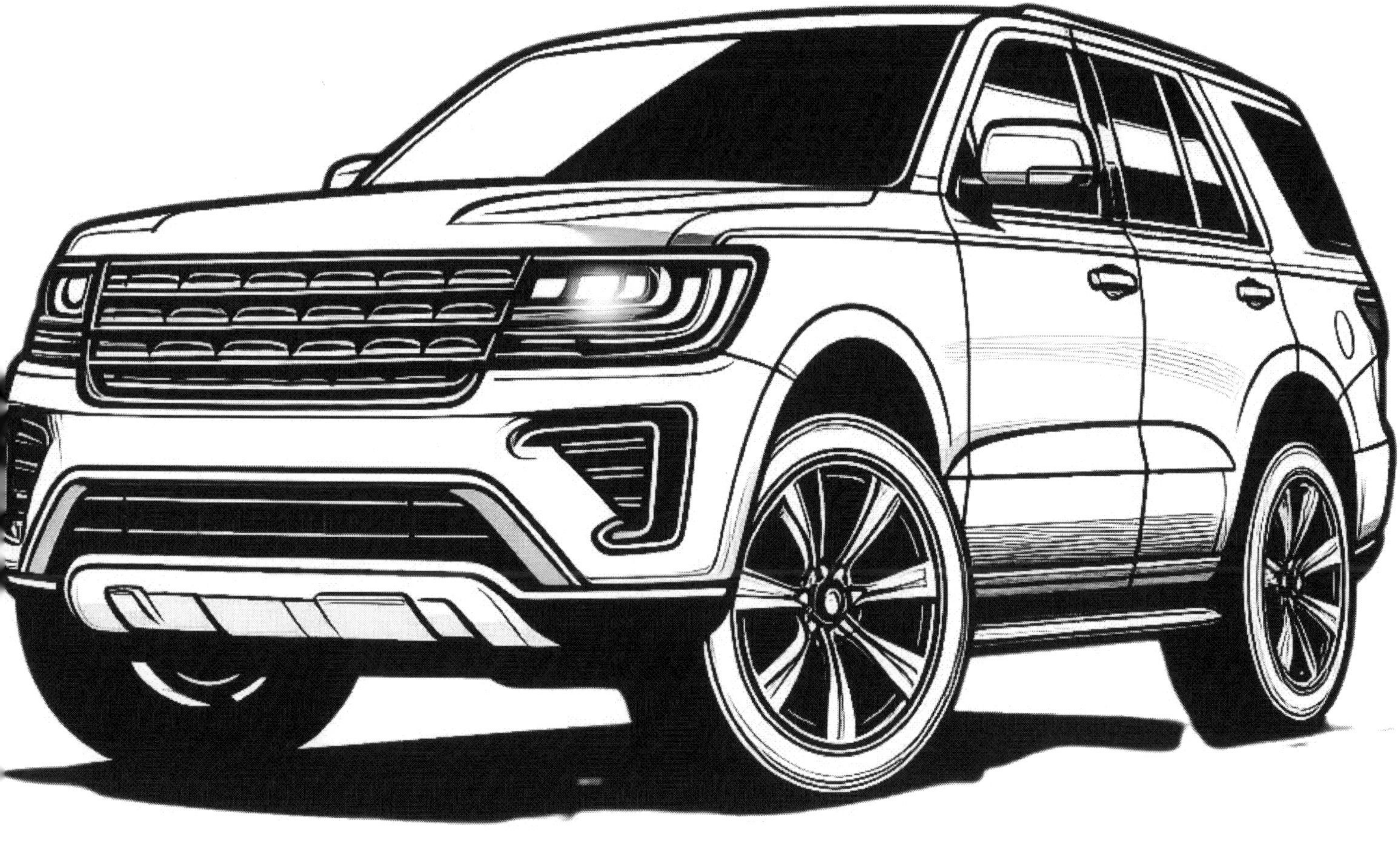

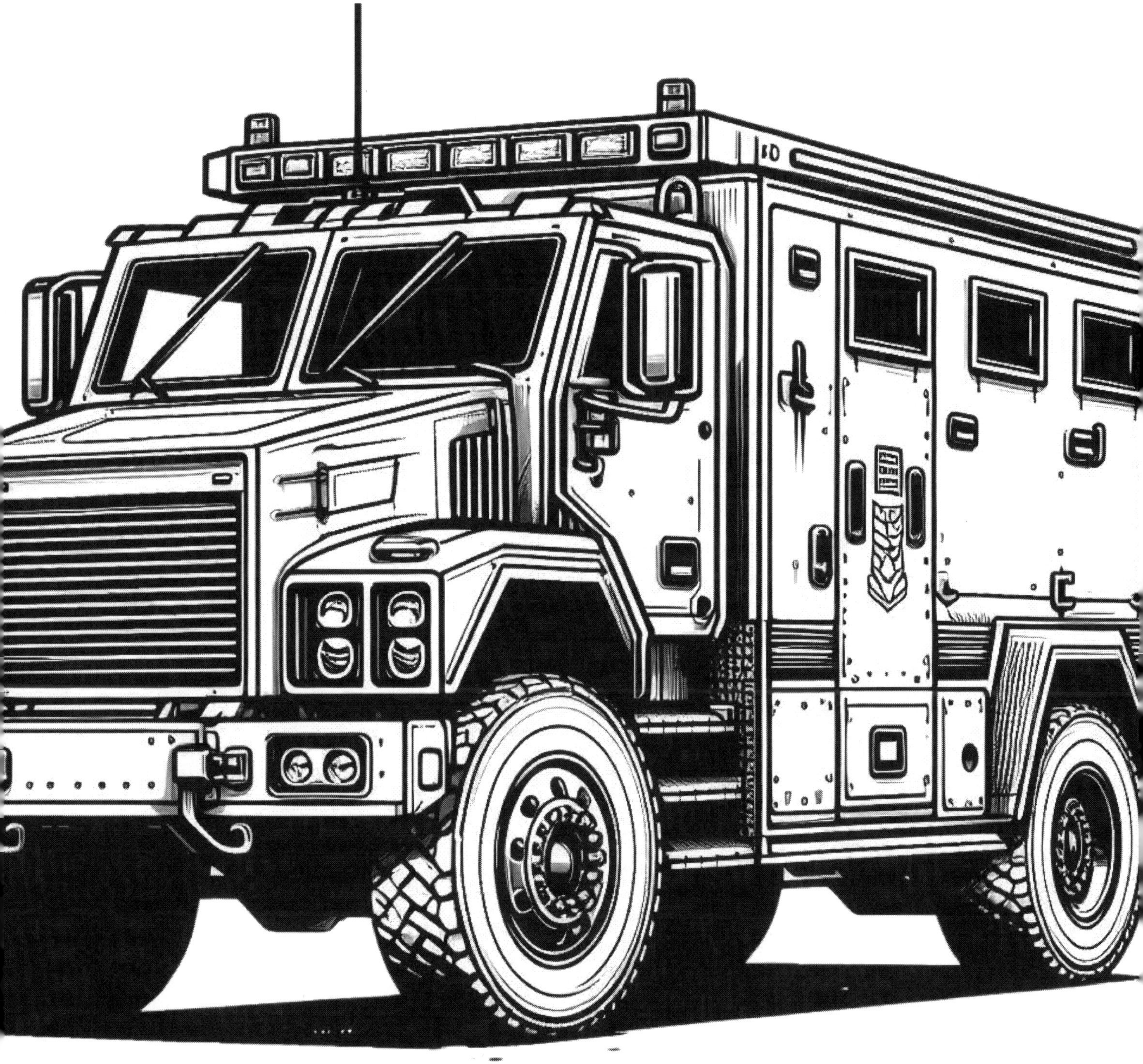

Made in the USA
Columbia, SC
25 November 2024